A CHILD LEFT BEHIND BY

Suicide

FROM DARKNESS TO GOD'S LIGHT

Mia Wallace

A Child Left Behind By Suicide
From Darkness to God's Light
By Mia Wallace

Printed in the United States of American

ISBN No. 978-0-578-51936-4

Kingdom Powerhouse LLC

In loving memory of those who have fallen by suicide.

You are truly missed and loved.

Your battle is not over, and honor will be brought to your name.

May God continue to shine His light on the darkness of suicide.

Rest in His loving peace until we are all join again.

Love, Mia Wallace

This book is dedicated to my Brothers & Sisters in Christ

Who have lost a loved one to suicide; and/or

To those who battle against the warfare of suicide.

May God send you the peace, love, comfort, and weapons

You need to carry out His mission for

This battle and its aftermath.

CONTENTS

"I am the light of the world.

He who follows Me shall not walk in darkness,

But have the light of life."

Jesus Christ

John 8:12

INTRODUCTION

The people who walked in darkness

Have seen a great light;

Those who dwelt in the land of the shadow of death,

Upon them a light has shined.

Isaiah 9:2

Life has away of giving us opportunities to share light from our own personal experiences with darkness. Though there are various forms of darkness in which we will encounter during our lifetime. We must remember the significance in the light, which has shined upon us, as we venture through our lives.

Luke 1:79 states that *John the Baptist came to give light to those who sit in darkness and the shadow of death, to guide our feet into the way of peace, and to prepare for the Lord's ways.* I believe we are to do the same with the light that has been given to us for those who are assigned to our lives.

I will be sharing my experience with overcoming and healing from the darkness of my childhood trauma. A trauma that is rapidly rising across the world and leaving many people trapped and mentally imprisoned after an encounter with suicide. My trauma came with a parent's suicide. Although there are many factors that should be considered with suicide, as a child who lost a parent in this manner it is extremely complicated at times to comprehend any reason for being left by this unfortunate circumstance.

As a child left behind by suicide, you are faced with many speculations about a person who is a part of your creation and existence. This was someone who you expected to be there to provide, protect, and care for you. As well as the person who would give you unconditional love and support throughout your life. Instead, you are left with no explanation, understanding, or guidance to process and accept this loss.

Shame, Fear, Depression, and Death become some of the many prison guards that hold you captive. You often do not know how to grieve the loss, which leaves you with multiple emotional issues and challenges that the enemy uses as barriers to prevent you from fully experiencing God's love. A love that is meant for all of His children including our fallen loved ones.

This book will equip you with the understanding of what you will need to be confident about your loved one's decision and God's unconditional love for us all. It can also be used as a source for other suicide loss survivors looking for comfort and peace; as well as a tool for suicide prevention, for those battling against suicide.

There are many obstacles associated with suicide and the aftermath of suicide. Those associations will only lead a person down to a pit of darkness. God has revealed His amazing light to the darkness of suicide, and His will to release those who are imprisoned mentally and emotionally due to suicide in this book.

Brothers and Sisters,
We do not want you to be uninformed about
those who sleep in death, so that you do not grieve
like the rest of mankind, who have no hope. For we
believe that Jesus died and rose again, and so we believe that
God will bring with Jesus those who have fallen asleep in him.

1 Thessalonian 4:13-14 (NIV)

CHAPTER 1

THE JOURNEY

By His light I walked through darkness

Job 29:3

Y ou are on a path to your favorite place in the world. You have been there millions of times and you thought you knew all the possible routes to get you there like the back of your hand. However, on one particular day you must have made a wrong turn or two along the way; because now you are stuck in a tunnel of complete darkness and you cannot find your way out.

You begin to panic, and the emotions of frustration, loneliness, and fear start to consume you and your thoughts. Those emotions begin to alter your decision-making skills. Each decision you make fails you and only leads you deeper into darkness.

As time goes on, you tell yourself this is all my fault; I deserve this; I am to blame; if only I did this or that differently, I would have never gotten stuck in this tunnel. After that session is over you tell yourself to just forget it. I would rather stay in this darkness; no one cares about me, or even loves me; they are not even searching for me. I give up! That is not even my favorite place anymore.

You begin to believe that being in darkness is where you were destined to be, but deep down inside of your heart you know this is not where you are supposed to be or belong. All of those lies that once comforted you, are no longer comforting and you feel the destruction that it's weighing on you.

Your soul will not let you settle, even though you keep telling yourself that it will be fine to stay in this darkness. You can no longer fight against your soul and body, so your mind starts to join them, and a sense of peace begins to take over you. Even though there is a peace, confusion of the mind begins to step in because nothing has changed in this darkness. This peace that you are sensing encourages you to stand still and embrace this darkness.

You no longer feel alone, and you notice a sparkle of light in the distance. A light which seems to have always been there. You just overlooked the light because you were focus on getting out of the tunnel your way. There is a drawing effect between you and the light: as you draw nearer to the light, the light draws nearer to you. As you hold onto this light, there is an over-whelming sense of love that comes over you as the light guides you through the darkness and out of the tunnel to something greater than you could have ever imagine.

This is my vision of our journeys of life. Jesus Christ is the sparkle of light which leads us out of the tunnels of darkness, that life can bring upon us to the great love of God. I pray that as you read about my journey you will receive what is meant for you and your journey of life.

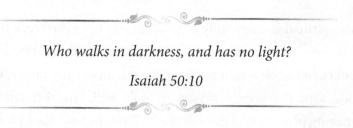

Who walks in darkness, and has no light?

Isaiah 50:10

A journey can be defined as an act or instance of traveling; or something suggesting travel or passage from one place to another. When it comes to defining a spiritual journey, it can only be defined as an experience of observing, seeking, and finding oneself on its highest level of creation through our one true creator. Although there are countless meanings of a spiritual journey, there is one fact which applies to them all.

The fact is you will be led to experience this journey from a higher source of power. I truly believe our spiritual journeys began from different points in our lives. These points typically stem from some type of darkness which crept onto our path. It is usually something that leaves us with an extreme pain, emotion, or situation with an unknown ending or outcome.

The unknown is what really makes us believe there is no light for us or our lives. This becomes an obstacle for the journey which is meant for us; because we cannot seem to get past the lesson that is assign to the darkness. I have come to the understanding that no matter how the darkness came in our way, whether it be from our actions or some other source, God will use it to teach us a lesson. He will bring glory and light to the darkness regardless as to how it originated onto our path of life.

My spiritual journey truly began after a major heartbreak from a seven-year relationship. I thought that since I prayed for someone to come into my life after the loss of my father; that God sent the perfect person to walk with me through the grieving process, and provide me at that time with the love that I deeply desired. When this was not the case, I was consumed with an unmeasurable amount of darkness, not only from the heartbreak of losing my first true love, my father; but also, the loss of a person that was extremely important to me for several years.

Unfortunately, we cannot prevent these times of being consumed by darkness from occurring in our lives. However, we can remember to seek and allow the amazing light to guide us through it. This light will present understanding and clarity of the lesson, as well as a higher perspective on the entire experience in which we are encountering in this particular season of our life.

The lesson learned from this darkness was that the enemy will send a counterfeit of what God has for us and what we truly want and desire before God deems time for us to have it. Especially, when it is something that only He can provide during these times of loss. I also realized that God was sending me major and significant warnings, signs, or whatever you would prefer to call them; which clearly showed and identified that this person was not sent by Him. It was an actual counterfeit sent to keep me stuck on my path of darkness.

Since I was not in strong relationship with God at the time, nor in His word, or seeking Him I was placed in a wilderness season of pain. This season put me at my lowest point. I was consumed by all types of troubles from all aspects of my life. I was trying very hard to settle in this place with numbness to all that was happening to me, but I got to a point where I could no longer deal with this on my own. Here is where my body, mind, and soul began to join; and the sparkle of light from the Lord came to get me out of this state of darkness, and heal my broken heart.

Often times the mind and body believes that it knows what is best for us; and we leave out the most important part of ourselves in the equation during critical times. We don't realize or remember that our soul is equipped with everything we need to survive this life. It knows exactly when to led us to the source to begin the spiritual journey required for us in this lifetime.

I will bring the blind by a way they did not know;

I will lead them in paths they have not known.

I will make darkness light before them,
and crooked places straight.

These things I will do for them,

And not forsake them.

Isaiah 42:16

Turning to God for His healing changed my season, it elevated my life on so many levels. Finally, I was in this amazing place on my spiritual journey. I was walking by His word, in His will, and chasing His amazing atmospheres at every conference and event that I could get to across the entire country.

Then things took a major turn for me. I was at one of these amazing conferences, and the Holy Spirit decided to single me out amongst the entire audience through one of the speakers whose session was on endangered hearts. The Holy Spirit revealed my truth that I lived my life imprisoned: an imprisonment which kept me in denial of my true self.

Initially, I was shocked when the speaker spoke on this matter of my life; and it was not because this was coming from a complete stranger in a room full of people that I did not know. I was shocked because it was true, and I felt a little exposed about that fact to say the least.

I lived in denial of my truth for so long that I even forgot this part of my life story even existed. Well, not really forgotten, but I just preferred that it was not a part of my truth. For the ones around me that knew about this truth, great; and to those that did not, even better for me, and my denial walk.

I found a way to live comfortably in my darkness by avoiding my truth and turning away from the light that was provided specifically for me. However, I could no longer find comfort and peace in my darkness as my denial was weighing heavily on my mind, body, and soul as I tried to settle in my darkness.

This was the point where my spiritual journey really turned real. It was taking me to a new level which required me to allow God to reveal His light to my darkness; and send His supernatural healing to me. As we built an intimate relationship together for my journey. This was all a part of God's plan to send His Holy Spirit to come and set me free from my imprisonment. John 16:13 tells us that *the Spirit of Truth, has come, He will guide you into all truth; for He will not speak on His own authority, but whatever He hears He will speak; and He will tell you things to come.*

Here is my truth, for thirty-one years I had been a prisoner to my childhood trauma with a gigantic prison guard named Death. At the age of four my mother committed suicide, within moments of me asking her one simple question, which my grandmother sent me to ask "do you want something to eat".

Shortly, before going to ask her that question I was super excited; because my grandmother had sent me on my own little mission to take charge with her authority. As I turned out of the room screaming down the hall while skipping to my own beat saying, "she said no, she said no grandma."

I was very proud of accomplishing my mission, and I was headed to find my next family member to ask them the same question. However, I was suddenly interrupted by the most terrifying sound. It was the loudest boom of my four years of life that stopped me right in my tracks. I stood there in the hallway frozen.

Something in me sensed that this was something bad, and it terrified me to move from my spot. I watched every one that was in the house run pass me and as they entered the room that my mother was in, they began to cry or scream. I was trying to figure out if I did something wrong as I stood there in the hallway because I was the last person to come out of that room.

Then I heard someone said get Mia, and I was rushed to the basement. I sat on a couch in the basement alone and just listened to the commotion that took place above me that left me lost and confused. I do not remember too much more from that day, mostly because of unhealthy grieving, lack of discussion, and lack of knowledge on the entire situation. I just know that was the day that I was sentenced to thirty-one years to prison; and became a lifetime prey to an endangered heart, and haunted by death.

As life went on, I was able to suppress my feelings and my thoughts all those years by blanking out my mother. This included not thinking or talking about her, or her actions. In my world, she no longer existed to me. I truly felt this was the best and only way to protect myself and other family members that suffered from her loss.

There were occasions when I did think or focused my attention to someone who was speaking about her which only left me with feelings of anger, shame, fear, worry, resentment, abandonment, unworthiness, sadness, and more depending on my age at the time. There were even times when I thought about how my life would have turned out if this never occurred. However, I was always able to shake those moments and thoughts off very quickly and proceed without her existence until now. My soul was leading the way, as my mind and body followed along this path.

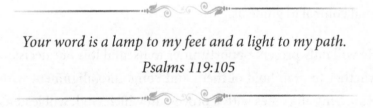

Your word is a lamp to my feet and a light to my path.
Psalms 119:105

When I made the decision to give my life to Christ and walk in His will completely, this is when the Holy Spirit also revealed to me at the same conference that I had to go back and get the little girl from my childhood who was left on the basement couch. I was told that she must go on this spiritual journey with me.

This journey consisted of a process in which God had to take me through in order to heal completely; and accept His truth which led me to His light and love for this unfortunate circumstance that took place in my life. I will be sharing all of this with you in this book.

I truly believe God will lead us through several journeys during our lifetime, and we are fortunate to have the opportunity to embrace Him along the way. We will choose various paths that will lead us to a positive or negative destination; and with God by our side, we are able to fully enjoy the positive and withstand all that comes with the negative.

Psalms 48:14 states *"for this is God our God forever and ever; He will be our guide even to death."* We must allow God to be our God. I know it is hard to turn over the free will that keeps us in control. However, God will only guide us through this life and, the warfare that comes with it; when we are willing to give Him total control to guide us.

He will only present opportunities to us, and it is our decision whether to grab hold of them and come into alignment with Him. This all comes with a process in which God, will lead us to the only path that really matters for our journey and His Kingdom.

I pray that as you read through this book that God will open your eyes, so that you can see His vision; open your ears, so that you can hear His voice; and open your heart, so you can receive all that He has for you; as you read along of this journey; in Jesus name I pray. Amen.

For I know the plans I have for you, declares the Lord, "plans to prosper you and not harm you, plans to give you hope and a future. Then you will call on me and come and pray to me, and I will listen to you. You will seek me and find me when you seek me with all your heart. I will be found by you," declares the Lord, and will bring you back from captivity.

Jeremiah 29:11-14 (NIV)

CHAPTER 2

THE PROCESS

When I sit in darkness, The Lord will be a light to me.

Micah 7:8

A process is a natural phenomenon marked by gradual changes that lead toward a particular result, with a series of actions or continuous operations to the end. With any journey, there is a process in which we must go through in order to get to our next level or path. Often, we delay, alter, and even miss out on key stops and attractions; because we wanted to bypass the process, so we can reach our desired destination immediately.

I believe there are multiple processes that are necessary and meant for us. These processes will develop and transform us throughout our lifetime. Our paths are destined and regardless to our decisions we must, and will venture through them.

For I consider that the sufferings of this present
time are not worthy to be compared with the
Glory which shall be revealed in us.

Romans 8:18

This process in which God had taken me through has been one of the hardest and heaviest things in which I had to face and address. It had always been my practice to avoid this part of my life and keep it tucked away. So naturally, it felt like I was going against myself and my plan for protection.

I had to constantly remind myself throughout this process that this was for the Lord's Kingdom; and His purpose to shed light to His children battling against suicide and its aftermath. Suicide is one of the leading causes of death throughout the entire world. As a loss survivor, you are faced with all types of emotions and left with a lot that is unknown, unanswered, and unaddressed.

This can push you deeper into a hopeless dark place. A place that can change your whole existence and consume you with a life of darkness, not just a wilderness season. Living a life in darkness is never a plan of God. This includes the times when we put ourselves or are placed in unfortunate situations that can cause many troubles and consequences for us. Please know we are not meant to live our lives in darkness.

This is just a way to blind us from what God has planned for us and our lives when we focus on our current circumstances. We must understand the meaning of what the darkness is meant to do to us. It is meant to keep us blinded, in a constant troubled state of living, and to keep us off the path that was created for us. A path that was created for us to live our lives amongst the light and shine the light which lives within us.

Darkness has its mission, but so does our light. Our current circumstances and situations were placed on our path for a specific reason. Even when we do not understand the reasoning for this experience; we will get through it and overcome this time. God has a unique way of transforming these times into something amazing for His Kingdom.

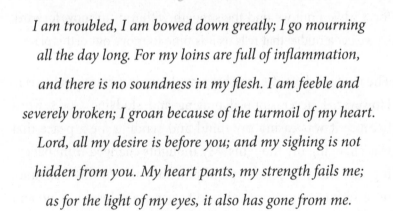

I am troubled, I am bowed down greatly; I go mourning all the day long. For my loins are full of inflammation, and there is no soundness in my flesh. I am feeble and severely broken; I groan because of the turmoil of my heart. Lord, all my desire is before you; and my sighing is not hidden from you. My heart pants, my strength fails me; as for the light of my eyes, it also has gone from me.

Psalms 38:6-10

When my imprisonment to this trauma was exposed, I felt completely heartbroken, lonely, and depressed. I thought my spiritual journey was moving along very well. I was seeking the Lord and chasing His amazing atmospheres. Now it seemed so overwhelming and a major block has been placed in front of me to halt my journey.

It appeared as if I was being tortured by doing the right thing, and desiring a relationship and purpose with the Lord. It is kind of ironic how the tunnels of darkness can just pop up into our lives. We can be traveling on the ultimate high of our life. Enjoying the path, we are on; and then suddenly, there is one change of event that pushes us into a tunnel of darkness.

Some events are minor and some are very major, but either way we get moved and knocked off our path. We even get stuck there for a while until we find the strength within us to move forward, or we get a nudge that tells us it is time to move out of this place.

The next six days after my big reveal I was an emotional wreck. However, I never stopped praying and studying God's word because it was easing my mind and sending me a peace that was changing my thoughts. My thoughts changed from believing that this was some type of punishment. To this was more necessary to move forward, and to get even closer to God and His mission.

This process taught me to worship in my pain. It pushed me forward, and motivated me to reach another level for what God was preparing within me; and for me to accomplish for Him.

I was not sure what He was preparing me for, but it definitely moved me out of my stuck place. A place that I had happen to be in for a few weeks.

Sometimes it is much easier to assume that the things that are happening to us is an act of the enemy or some form of punishment from God. This is usually because it is something that we disagree with, its not pleasing to our flesh, or there is some misunderstanding of it. However, we must understand that there will always be something like this occurring in our lives, and it is okay.

Overall, I am finding it is best to view this as something necessary for us, and it is something we must go through in order to be the person that we were created to be in this world. There is a process to become the image that God created us to be; and we must be willing to become that image by all means necessary for our journeys.

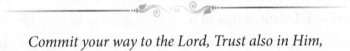

Commit your way to the Lord, Trust also in Him,

And He shall bring it to pass. He shall bring forth your

righteousness as the light, and your justice as the noonday.

Psalms 37:5-6

I know all of that sounded perfect and simple, but I also know there is still some resistance to the process. I tried very hard to resist what God was processing in my life. I truly did not want any part of this, but that heavy burden was blocking my path. I knew that God was the only one that could and would clear my way, but I was still resisting what He was doing in my life.

After trying to resist this process for several weeks. The Lord sat me down and let me know that I needed to release this trauma. I was in disbelief that God wanted me to face this trauma. On days that I wanted to ignore this entire situation, He would present the subject to me through others from testimonies at church on their suicide attempts, preachings or sermons that I would listen to, television shows or movies I watched, and even random articles that I would come across.

I could not escape or run away from the subject of suicide no matter what I tried to do to avoid it. I thought I had done very well with blocking it out and functioning as if it never occurred or existed. I wanted this to be over as quickly as possible, but rushing the process is never the way to go and it actually adds unnecessary delays and additional paths that God never intended for us to take. We also miss the importance in what the process is instilling in us when we rush through it.

Of course, I had to learn all of this the hard way because I still tried to rush through my process. By trying to rush through and seek my own quick way through this process without God's counsel. I interpreted the "go back and get the little girl from my childhood" from the Holy Spirit as you need to go back and remember everything that you can; and figure out all of the details of what happened with my mother, as the way to get that little girl from my childhood back.

I began to search for details, and became overwhelmed. I really did not know what I was looking for; or had anyone around who I felt comfortable with to explain, answer my questions, or provide me with the comfort to accept this as part of my life. I was extremely frustrated with myself. I felt like I should have remembered something since I was there.

I put extra stress and tension on myself. In my mind, I truly thought that I should have remembered what happen. I made those details a requirement for this journey. I even unknowingly turned to unauthorized counsels that only deepen my darkness and caused confusion, distraction, and separation towards other loved ones in my life.

The enemy played all of this against me. I focused so much on remembering and finding details. That once I could not find what I was seeking. My thoughts turned into nothing but negativity. I even had an internal mental abuse session or rather, an abusive match with myself. I thought that I needed to conqueror all of this on my own, which made me feel disheartened, disappointed, and a complete failure.

I was getting dragged deeper into my darkness as each day went by because I was not moving forward. I was stuck in this hopeless spot on my path. All of this was another level on my spiritual journey. The Lord was teaching me that He was in control over this matter; and that I needed to surrender all of this to Him. I needed to allow him to work His supernatural healing on my heart, and life to bring light to my darkness.

This had definitely changed me. I was so vulnerable and exposed to the point where I had to trust the Lord; and have faith in Him during this time and season. I may not understand the whole process or the entire lesson, which was taking place, but I had to believe in God's light because all I could see and feel was the darkness that was consuming my life.

All the paths of the Lord are mercy and truth

Psalms 25:10

Once I embraced God and held onto Him for my strength. He began to lead me out of my isolation season. A season of only wanting to be by myself in the comfort of my own space. I felt like there was no one out there in the world who could truly relate to what I was going through; or provide me with what I needed and wanted at that time. Truthfully, I could not even explain what I wanted or needed to anyone, even if I tried.

The enemy enjoyed my season of isolation. He threw many lies my way and tried his hardest to keep me in the darkness. But I held onto that strength that God provides to us all to weather through those thoughts and feelings that comes with the darkness. He started putting me right where I needed to be to move forward on this path.

I was being placed in new environments. While God orchestrated the perfect encounters with individuals, that would assist with different parts of my healing. At this point, I was ready to be healed, face all my fears, and accept the status of being a suicide loss survivor. I was tired of carrying this heaviness with me. It was time for me to move to the path of healing.

To everything there is a season, A time for every purpose under heaven: A time to be born, and a time to die; A time to plant, and a time to pluck what is planted; A time to kill, and a time to heal; A time to break down, and a time to build up; A time to weep, and a time to laugh; A time to mourn, and a time to dance; A time to cast away stones, and time to gather stones; A time to embrace, and a time to refine from embracing; A time to gain, and a time to lose; A time to keep, and a time to throw away; A time to tear, and a time to sew; A time to keep silence, and a time to speak; A time to love, and a time to hate; A time of war, and a time of peace.

Ecclesiastes 3:1-8

CHAPTER 3

THE HEALING

For it is the God who commanded light to shine out of darkness, who has shone in our hearts to give the light of the knowledge of the Glory of God in the face of Jesus Christ

2 Corinthians 4:6

In the beginning of my spiritual walk, I kept hearing many leaders speak on the fact that everyone has a purpose in God. I always wondered what my purpose was from the very first moment of hearing it. I began to ask the Lord what was my purpose and how will He use me. I had no idea it would have anything to do with dealing with this part of my life.

However, I felt like now that I know my purpose or a least one of my purposes and assignments. It was time to take action; but God put a quick stop to that. He said it was time to heal first. You cannot share what you have not received. You cannot bring light to this trauma until you allow Me to bring light to your trauma. This required me to become whole and allow God to have total control over my life.

For this very purpose I have raised you up, that
I may show My power in you, and that My
name may be declared in all the earth.

Romans 9:17

The path of healing is the path of becoming whole in God. We often believe we are healed from circumstances and situations which have taken place in our lives without God; because it feels as if we are moving along just fine on our paths with the hurt. However, it is more than likely a false sense of I can move forward, because I suppressed the pain. So it does not affect my outer appearance and my inner core has become numb to the aching which has taken place from this hurt.

We do not consider the root that is buried deep inside of us that holds all that is associated to this pain. This root is what really prevents us from moving forward to our ordained destinations. In order to be fully healed; this root must be uprooted. God is the only one who can uproot and heal the roots of life. This is one of many reasons why we should give God complete access to our lives. So He can do His work on us, and through us to become the godly vessels he needs in this world.

Although, I understood this; it was much easier to say than to do. It became a daily battle of releasing my emotions and thoughts to God through praying and believing. After a period of time, I added fasting to the mix. I fasted for greater understanding of what was going on with me; answers for questions that only God could reveal to me, and for more clarity to the meaning of what is meant for my life. God is the only source for us. We are responsible for our own healing and going to the source to heal all matters of our lives.

In order for me to accept the action that my mother took I had to turn to my source, who would provide me with a way to accept it without allowing it to define me and my purpose that He has specifically for me. Jeremiah 33:6 states "*I will bring it health and healing; I will heal them and reveal to them the abundance of peace and truth*".

*Trust in the Lord with all your heart, and
lean not on your own understanding;*

*In all your ways acknowledge Him and
He shall direct your paths.*

Proverbs 3:5-6

When we lean on our own understanding, we redirect ourselves away from the journey; which we should be traveling through for our kingdom mission. God has to direct our paths on this journey, so we can fulfill and accomplish His will for our lives. This is the importance of acknowledging Him in all our ways as the scripture states. God only knows the true calling on our lives; so we must trust Him to direct us through these journeys of life.

I misinterpreted what was required of me through the message that I received from the Holy Spirit. I assumed that I needed to go back to my childhood and relive through all the pain and confusion. When in actuality, God was saying you need to acknowledge what happened and accept it as a part of my true story. We must own our truth and everything that contributes to who we are in this life.

God will give us the strength to overcome the traumas, prisons, guards, people, etc., as well as anything else which contributes to our captivities. In my case, He was telling me there was no need for me to know the details of everything that occurred with my mother and her situation. God kept all of it from me for a reason.

He showed me who was in control over this matter when it pertained to me and my safety. God protected me when I was young, innocent, and vulnerable to what was happening during this situation. God knew all of those details, and that is all that really mattered. He wanted me to forgive. I needed to forgive. I had to forgive. I forgave my mother, my father, myself, and whoever else I truly felt in my heart needed to be forgiven for the sake of this matter.

After forgiveness, the next step to my healing was to face the truth of my unknown story. The truth was very simple, to say the least, it was the fact that I did not have to seek the details of my loss, rather seek God in my story. It was necessary for me to change my focus on how I would bring out the light in which God purposely placed as my mission for His Kingdom through my story.

In order to walk with the Lord, I had to own my truth. I must always walk in this truth! This was the light in which the Lord was going to use for other children living in denial like myself or shamed by their accounts with suicide. The time has come to shine light and knowledge on the darkness of suicide.

God provides us with numerous gifts. I am truly blessed to have received a few that can be used to connect me with others on many levels and adapt to various environments. I believe it is to share this miraculous story of healing and God's supernatural healing from an unknown circumstance; that was meant to steal, kill, and destroy me, and my sisters and brothers in Christ.

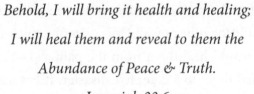

Behold, I will bring it health and healing;
I will heal them and reveal to them the
Abundance of Peace & Truth.
Jeremiah 33:6

On this journey, I found comfort and understanding in a few books, some research I did, and other materials on the effects of suicide loss. I wanted to share some important points, facts, encouraging words, etc. and state how they affected me directly. Along with comforting scriptures of the Lord's loving words that can secure you in the time of revealing and releasing as part of the healing.

The two main books that I will be referencing in this section are listed below. I will quote directly from these books and place the number of the reference in parenthesis after each quotation.

I. Blindsided by Suicide by Linda Kipley

II. The Wounded Child's Journey into Love's Embrace by Paul Ferrini

"My foundation with Christ as the Cornerstone in my life carried me through. He not only carried me, but also overtime as I continued to trust Him, He began to bring healing and restoration." (I)

I witnessed the destruction that a broken heart can cause in a person's life. The person in most of those cases turned to an addiction add/or other means for a simple quick fix or any-thing that would heal them from the pain as fast as possible. This only led them to a complete disaster. It is such a tragedy to watch a person, especially a loved one live their life in complete darkness, and self-destruction due to a broken heart or for any reason to avoid the pains of their life.

This was one of the generational curses on my family. This curse came for me, but I turned to the real source of healing and broke this curse by turning to God; and going through His process of healing that only He can implement into our lives. Turning to Christ during my heartbreak was the start to building a true foundation with him.

Trusting God with this most vulnerable part of my life was the start to building an intimate relationship with him. This has brought healing and restoration to the darkness that has been shadowing me and holding me captive throughout my life. We have to really believe that God can use our experiences of life, and make some good out of it. He will turn our experience into a template or even better, a master plan for others that may face similar barriers on their paths.

> *"My inner child wanted to be told one minute "I Love You" and then the next moment pushed away. He wanted consistency, not emotional push-pull. "I Love You, but won't you please go away" is a difficult message for any child to hear." (II)*

This touched me so deeply because I treated my inner child like this for many years. I truly abandoned the little girl from my childhood, which is so heartbreaking. She was innocent and confused about everything that was taking place in her life during this time. I left and ignored her needs. She needed to feel safe to express her emotions instead of being forced to suppress them. My inner child wanted unconditional love rather than loved on the conditions of being hidden and pushed away.

This is how I contributed to my dysfunctional/emotional health and abandonment issues. This was one of the hidden problems that I had with myself that was revealed to me during one of my fast. I eventually had to forgive myself in order for my inner child and adult self to join back together with unconditional love for one another to complete this journey.

This is what the Holy Spirit wanted me to do with the statement to go back and get the little girl from my childhood, because she must to go on this journey with me. We must be completely whole for our journeys and all parts of ourselves must be joined together and healed to move forward with the Lord.

> *"All I can do about the past is forgive myself and you for the Love we were unable to give. And all that I can do about the future is release my expectations which limit it and hold it hostage to the past." (II)*

> *"Suicide is such an unexpected and violent end to a life, robbing our loved ones of all God has for them on this earth. I believe God is omnipotent and omnipresent. I believe God never makes a mistake." (I)*

I agree with Mrs. Kipley. God is omnipotent, omnipresent and never makes a mistake. I also know that God gives us free will over our lives. He will not make us do anything that we do not want to do. We have the choice to do whatever, we choose to do for ourselves.

This meant that I could not blame God for allowing this to happen, because this was my mother's decision. I truly believe that

He was present with her pleading for her to trust Him, and that He was handling her situation if only she would have chosen him to have complete control over her situation. As Paul Ferrini stated in the quote above all I can do about the past is forgive and all I can do about the future is release my expectations, so the past is not held hostage within it my future.

The book *Conversations with God-an uncommon dialogue, Book 1* by Neale Donald Walsch quotes that "the Spirit will never, ever, force His desire on the present, conscious, physical part of you. The Father will not force His will upon the Son. It is violation of His very nature to do so, and thus, quite literally, impossible. The Son will not force His will upon the Holy Spirit. It is against His very nature to do so, and thus, quite literally impossible. The Holy Spirit will not force His will upon your soul. It is outside of the nature of the Spirit to do so, and thus, quite literally, impossible.

Here is where the impossibilities end. The mind very often does seek to exert its will on the body-and actually does so. Similarly, the body seeks often to control the mind-and frequently succeeds. Yet the body and the mind together do not have to do anything to control the soul - for the soul is completely without need (unlikely the body and the mind, which are shackled with it), and so allows the body and the mind to have their way all the time."

This gives us an understanding of how much control we actually have over our lives. We must allow the Holy Spirit to move through us as our direct contact and connection to God.

He will only communicate God's will to us and never force it upon us. We have to make the ultimate decision whether to accept God's will or our will for our lives.

> *"Satan works hard at convincing loved ones left behind that they were to blame. More than ever we need to stay focused on God's truth. Christians are not exempt from tragic events storming into our lives." (I)*

This enemy was working hard to persuade me a four year old at the time; that I was to blame for my mother's action. As if I could have changed the outcome if only I did something differently that day. The enemy had me thinking throughout those thirty-one years that I was not enough or worth living for because my mother committed suicide. He also tried to manipulate me over the years to convince me that there was no point to my existence. This enemy wanted me to believe there was no hope in living; and that I could have a better life if I went and joined my mother in a place of peace and happiness, without the stress and drama of this life.

The thief does not come except to steal,
and to kill, and to destroy.

I have come that they may have life, and that
they may have it more abundantly.

John 10:10

This is the most important reason why we must focus on God's truth. God's truth will reveal and expose the lies of the enemy, so we do not fall victim to his traps, schemes, and prisons. John 8:32 says *you shall know the truth, and the truth shall make you free.* God's truth will bring us life; even when we feel and see nothing but death. Some may wonder what God's truth is, so let's discuss that briefly before moving on to the next quote.

In the article *Grace to You* by John MacArthur truth is define as "that which is consistent with the mind, will, character, glory, and being of God. It stated that truth is not subjective, it is not a consensual cultural construct, and it is not an invalid, outdated, irrelevant concept. It is the reality God has created and defined, and over which He rules.

To reject and rebel against the truth of God results in darkness, folly, sin, judgement, and the never-ending wrath of God. To accept and submit to the truth of God is to see clearly, to know with certainty and to find life everlasting." Now that is the wonders of God's truth.

>*"I still did not have the answers to my questions and realized it might take until eternity before I got them." (II)*

This is one of the issues that had me stuck in a hopeless place on my path. I was so concern about my unanswered questions and the unknown that I could not move forward. They became a distraction to what was answered and known. I knew that I had to accept this fact that my unanswered questions would not be answered, and the unknown would remain unknown.

However, what was known was that I would trust God to reveal and release what I need and when I need to know something. This gave and continues to give me comfort and security knowing that God is protecting me mentally and emotionally. I was able to move forward on knowing that God will protect and provide what is meant for me to succeed on this journey.

> *"More and more peace had settled over me as I surrendered the guilt, the shame, and the anger I was harboring in my heart. I chose to trust God's sovereign timing in life and death." (I)*

Surrendering has been a major and critical step in healing from this loss for me. In Billy Graham's message on total surrender he tells us that "if you want a change in your life, if you want forgiveness and peace and joy that you have never known before, God demands total surrender. He becomes the Lord and the ruler of your life."

It was not until I surrendered all of my emotions; and the unknown that was harboring in my heart to the Lord, that I could began to see the light. The heaviness that was hovering over my shoulders began to lift each day. As I trusted and believed in God's sovereign timing over the events that were taking place in those moments of surrendering different parts of myself. My path became clear once I surrendered all matters to our Lord and Savior; and gave Him total control over my life.

> *"I recognized the warm, healing touch of the Lord. He truly was aware of her death. He was there, God had*

allowed it for a reason. She was with him; I had no question in my mind about that the enemy would no longer be able to try to talk me out of what I heard. He allowed her death and would redeem it! He was always in charge, even in suicide." (I)

I truly believe that God is always in charge and will redeem us from our sins. There are many unknown factors involved with suicide, but as a loss survivor, we must find peace and light in the lives of our loved ones. Suicide to me is a weapon used in the spiritual warfare.

I know that the enemy believes, and wants us to believe that death has won the battle against our loved ones; but we must remember that our Lord and Savior Jesus Christ defeated death. We have to stand on this and know that God considers death an enemy that will be destroyed. 1 Corinthians 15:26 states that *the last enemy to be destroy is death.*

In Revelation 21:4 (NIV) it ensures us that *He will wipe every tear from their eyes. There will be no more death or mourning or crying or pain for the old order of things has passed away.* Trust in these truths and know that God is with us and our loved ones.

"There are times in our walk when God requires everything we have. The separation caused by suicide of a loved one certainly qualifies as one of those times. Separation from a loved one as a result of suicide needs to be addressed more in our society, especially our Christian

**Society. We as Survivors desperately need to the body
of Christ." (I)**

I feel there are occasions within the Christian Society when
individuals put more concentration on the appearance of being righteous and religious. This redirects the focus from what
truly matters to the meaning of the society. For example, with
suicide, there tends to be a judgmental view on how the person
died which becomes the focus. Instead of exemplifying Christ's
love in providing the love and support that is needed and required to the ones left behind by their death.

Death by suicide takes the loved ones left behind through a
very traumatic grieving process that builds up walls of horror,
shame, guilt, anger, confusion, and more overwhelming feelings that make you isolate yourself in a pit of darkness. As a
loss survivor, I am screaming across the entire world to all the
churches that are a part of the body of Christ that we need
the light of Jesus Christ that is within you all to shine bright
on the darkness of suicide.

O Lord my God, I cried out to you, and you healed me.

O Lord, You brought my soul up from the grave;

You kept me alive, that I should not go down to the pit.

Sing praise to the Lord, you saints of His, and give

thanks at the remembrance of His holy name

Psalms 30:2-4

I wanted to share the seven steps that I went through in my healing process. These steps assisted me through my breakthrough. I believe they are keys for many of the paths that we will travel along on our journeys. Here are the steps:

1. **Repentance:** I needed to first repent for my known and unknown sins and turn away from my wicked ways. This is something that I must do often because hey, I'm human. However, this is a very important step because our sins will make God hide His face from us. God does not listen to sinners, which is why this step is very critical for us. (John 9:31, Isaiah 59:2)

2. **Quietness:** It was important for me to have quiet time with God. We needed our much-needed alone time together. This step is a major part in the foundation of building an intimate relationship with God. During this time I was required to turn away from the world (no cell phone, tv, social media, people) and focus on what God placed on my heart for the day or I sat with God and either spoke or wrote what was on my heart, this included my frustrations, emotions, confusions, and my gratitude for His many blessings.

3. **Praying & Fasting:** This was significant to strengthen my communication skills with God. I learned how to really pray to God and allow the Holy Spirit within me to intercede in my prayers. It was no longer a time of praying for meaningless things and circumstances. During the times of fasting, I received answers, understanding, and more than I could have ever imagined on specific known and

unknown questions, requests, and situations that I needed His guidance, advice, or peace of mind on.

4. **Acceptance:** God will reveal so much when you get in alignment with Him, and sometimes your flesh will not want to conform or agree with what God is speaking and showing you. It is imperative that we accept the truth of the matters in our lives. I had to turn from resistances and embrace the truth that was being revealed for what it was-*God's truth.*

5. **Surrender:** Surrendering all matters to God with no expectation, outcome, or result in mind has been the best. Life has become much lighter and runs much smoother by just trusting God with everything and everyone. This is coming from a person who had, and still struggles at times with a habit of taking on everything; and feeling that it is my responsibility to handle and resolve everything for everyone.

6. **Forgiveness:** We are often not aware of the importance of forgiveness. It seems as a minor act, but I learnt from experience that unforgiveness comes with a lot of heavy negative baggage. The release that comes with forgiving makes space within for God to fill us with love and purpose for His kingdom. He can turn all things good, even when we do not see the good.

7. **Acknowledgment:** Acknowledging and believing in God for who He is as our God, His supernatural, His promises, and His love for us as His children. This has opened me

to accept my journey and to endure all that comes with it knowing that God is with me always.

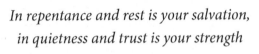

In repentance and rest is your salvation,
in quietness and trust is your strength

Isaiah 30:15 (NIV)

I will close this chapter with the importance of allowing ourselves the time needed to heal on our journeys. There is no set time, timetable, or time frame which can be used to determine the amount of time required for our healing. God works in His own sovereign timing over our lives.

He will not just heal us in one particular area that is currently affecting us, but rather heal us from our past and present hurts. God will heal the roots within us, which will take time. It really all depends on us, and our trust in God for our healing.

There will be times when it may seem as if there is nothing happening or being shifted in our favor. God is still working in those times. We must believe that in the end this is all for the good of our breakthrough. God is right there waiting on us to grab hold of Him. You will never be alone on this path of healing. God will always be there with you.

CHAPTER 4

THE GUARDS

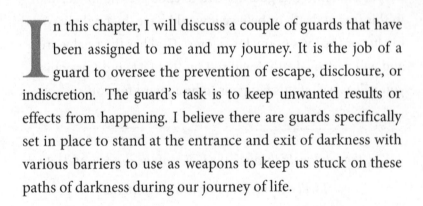

*He uncovers deep things out of darkness, and
brings the shadow of death to light*

Job 12:22

I n this chapter, I will discuss a couple of guards that have
been assigned to me and my journey. It is the job of a
guard to oversee the prevention of escape, disclosure, or
indiscretion. The guard's task is to keep unwanted results or
effects from happening. I believe there are guards specifically
set in place to stand at the entrance and exit of darkness with
various barriers to use as weapons to keep us stuck on these
paths of darkness during our journey of life.

One guard that has a major role with suicide and has had a major impact on me is called Death. Death is defined as the end of
life-the state of being no longer alive. It has a reputation of being

the final act of our lives and journeys. I believe its reputation is what tortures and stings many of us. The fact of no longer being here physically is hard to accept when you live only by flesh.

Although there are many guards associated with suicide and the traumas of life. Death was the guard that haunted me the most. I was terrified of death. I felt like I was walking around on eggshells wondering who will be the next to leave me or when will it be my turn to leave this world. This took placed for many years especially in my youth.

> "To a doctor or a nurse, death is failure. To a friend or relative, death is disaster. Only to the soul is death a relief or a release." ~Neale Donald Walsch

The quote above by Neale Donald Walsch added to my conviction that it was definitely time for me to face death and take a deeper look into this guard. I had to choose to no longer walk in this fear of death or believe it would have the final say over my life or the lives of my loved ones. God has the final word and will destroy death. I will rest on that fact, and I pray that you will as well if this happens to be a guard for you.

Yea, though I walk through the valley of the shadow of death,

I will fear no evil; For You are with me;

Your rod and Your staff, they comfort me.

Psalms 23:4

In the book *Conversations with God-an uncommon dialogue, Book 1* by Neale Donald Walsch; God mentions some very important understandings in his discussion that can give us comfort, peace, or just another perspective to ease our minds.

> *"You have created a society in which it is very not okay to want to die-very not okay with death. Because you don't want to die, you can't imagine anyone wanting to die-no matter what their circumstances or condition. But there are many situations in which death is preferable to life. Yet these truths don't occur to you they are not self-evident-when you are looking in the face of someone else who is choosing to die.*
>
> *When the soul makes the decision nothing the body does can change it. Nothing the mind thinks can alter it. If the soul is very clear that staying does not serve its higher agenda that there is no further way it can evolve through this body-the soul is going to leave and nothing will stop it nor should anything try to-its purpose is evolution. That is its sole purpose-and its soul purpose. The soul is clear that there is no great tragedy involved in leaving the body."*

I turned to the Bible for God's word, understanding, and perspective on death. I knew that fearing death was not a part of His plan for any of His children. I also knew the only way to overcome this guard would be to go to Him as my source of reference for my fears. The enemy wants us to believe that once we die that is the end and the final point to our existence.

However, John 3:16 states that *God so loved the world that he gave His only son that whoever believes in Him should not perish but have eternal life.* You read that correctly, we receive everlasting life through our Lord and Savior and there is no final point to our existence, if we believe in Him.

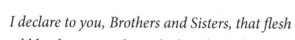

I declare to you, Brothers and Sisters, that flesh and blood cannot inherit the kingdom of God, nor does the perishable inherit the imperishable.

1 Corinthians 15:50 (NIV)

Paul tells us in 1 Corinthians 15:54 that when *"the perishable has been clothed with the imperishable, and the mortal with immortality, then that is written will come true "Death has been swallowed up in victory."* He also tells us in 1 Corinthian 15:58 (NIV):

Brothers and Sisters stand firm.

Let nothing move you.

Always give yourselves fully to the work of the Lord,

Because you know that your labor in the Lord is not in vain.

This is very comforting to know that our work in the Lord and our victories will contribute to the abolishment of death, as we live forever in the kingdom of God. Even with knowing this I still needed more understanding from God. I wanted and needed to know what and how God truly felt about the act of suicide.

According to the world, suicide is an unforgivable sin because "thou shall not kill" or whatever commandment it feels has been broken by this cause of death. However, the Lord has declared to us in Isaiah 55:8-9 that "*my thoughts are not your thoughts, neither are your ways my ways. As the heavens are higher than the earth, so are my ways higher than your ways and my thoughts than your thoughts.*"

As mentioned in a previous chapter suicide is a result of many factors and unfortunate circumstances that only God could place judgment over. We could never understand the uniquely design battle that is set in place for an individual. There is no way for anyone to fully be aware of the attacks associated with each battle a person face, especially those with an opponent such as suicide.

For we do not wrestle against flesh and blood, but against principalities, against powers, against the rulers of the darkness of this age, against spiritual hosts of wickedness in heavenly places.

Ephesians 6:12

It is extremely important that we keep hold to this when we are in judgmental environments, or encountering judgmental or very religious people. For some reason, there are many people who feel like they have to voice their opinion on suicide, and harshly judge and speak ignorantly on the subject with no consideration for those affected by this matter. For this reason, be sure to do the following:

Stand therefore, having girded your waist with truth, having put on the breastplate of righteous, and having shod your feet with the preparation of the gospel of peace, above all taking the shield of faith with which you will be able to quench all the fiery darts of the wicked one. And take the helmet of Salvation, and the Sword of the Spirit which is the word of God.

Ephesians 6:14-17

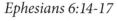

I will end the discussion on this guard with a quote from the book *Conversations with God-an uncommon dialogue, Book 2* by Neale Donald Walsch:

"First, understand that death is not an end, but a beginning; not a horror, but a joy. It is not a closing down, but an opening up. The happiest moment of your life will be the moment it ends. That is because it doesn't end but only goes on in ways so magnificent, so full of peace and wisdom and joy, as to make it difficult to describe and impossible for you to comprehend."

Shame is the next guard I will be discussing in this chapter. Shame was another guard that was before me, defined as a painful emotion caused by consciousness of guilt, shortcoming, or impropriety; and a deep personal humiliation or disgraceful/dishonorable conduct, quality, or action. I did not realize how much power shame could have over a person, until I evaluated my issues with shame.

The battles of life are never really over; and their attacks are just disguised differently as we conqueror and elevate from them along our journeys. Shame was one of the top reasons as to why I never spoke on my mother's suicide. It had this power over me to keep me in a place of silence. It brought out fears and misplaced emotions to bear in my darkness. This guard called Shame directed all of the burden on me.

In Dr. Stacey Freedenthal piece *Shame Fester in Dark Place: Keeping Suicide Secret*, she points out that when shame goes unchallenged in its darkness, it wins; and when undeserved shame is exposed to light, it weakens. Pastor John Piper the founder and teacher of desiringGod.org *Battling the Unbelief of Misplaced Shame* article shares with us that "the Bible makes very clear that there is a shame we ought to have and a shame we ought not to have.

He defines misplaced shame (the same as undeserved shame) as the shame you feel when there is no good reason or feel it. "Biblically, it means the thing you feel ashamed of is not dishonoring to God or that it is dishonoring to God, but you didn't have a hand in it. Pastor Piper also explains that if we want to battle shame at the root, we have to know how it relates to God because shame can cripple us if we do not know how to deal with them at the root.

Much of our shame is not God-centered, but self-centered and we are required to handle that fact in order to be able to battle the problem of shame at its root. Lastly, he teaches us that "by believing the promises of God all the efforts to put us to shame will fail in the end. We may struggle now to know what our shame is to bear and what is not. But God has promises for us:

Israel is saved by the Lord with everlasting salvation, you shall not be put to shame or confounded to all eternity.

Isaiah 45:17 (ESV)

Anyone who believes in him will never be put to shame.

Romans 10:11; 9:33 (NIV)

We have to battle our undeserved misplaced shame by understanding that it is not ours to bear, and for all the distress and spiritual warfare it brings, the promises stand sure that they will not succeed in the end."

Instead of your shame you shall have double honor,
and instead of confusion they shall rejoice in their
portion... Everlasting joy shall be theirs.

Isaiah 61:7

Guilt is the last guard that I would like to address in this chapter. As it relates to suicide, this guard has a major impact on an individual's mental state of processing their encounter properly. Guilt is defined as a state of one who has consciously committed an offense; as well as feelings of deserving blame, especially for imagined offenses or from a sense of inadequacy.

For those who live according to the flesh set their minds on the things of the flesh, but those who live according to the Spirit, the things of the Spirit. For to be carnally minded is death, but to be spiritually minded is life and peace.

Romans 8:5-6

Although, Guilt was not one of my guards, I witness the role that it had over a few of my family members. Guilt has its own way of tormenting an individual. It prevents and hinders the person from receiving the peace and joys of life. This can really become a huge struggle for a nonbeliever or an unfaithful believer because they are forced to carry this burden of blame with them throughout their life.

I want to make this known that all of the feelings of guilt and everything that is carried with the guilt can be put down and left in the hands of God. Guilt has a way of keeping us from believing that we deserve to be in the will of God or even worst be in any type of relationship with him due to some wrong doing, which has settled in our thoughts.

It wants us to journey through life on this destructive self-condemned path, which is the complete opposite of what God has planned for our journeys.

John 3:17-18 tells us that *for God did not send His Son into the world to condemn the world, but that the world through Him might be saved. He who believes in Him is not condemned; but he who does not believe is condemned already, because he has not believed in the name of the only begotten Son of God.* We are reminded in Romans 8:1 that *there is no condemnation to those who are in Christ Jesus, who do not walk according to the flesh, but according to the Spirit.*

When we chose to believe in our Lord and Savior Jesus Christ, the condemnation of this world; which includes self-condemnation is removed from our path. We are able to journey through life knowing that we have been rescued and saved from this state of living.

Now may the God of hope fill you with all joy

and peace in believing, that you may abound

in hope by the power of the Holy Spirit.

Romans 15:13

In order to be released from any guard you must face and expose it. Death, Shame, and Guilt are just a few of the guards that was discussed in this book. However, there are many guards associated with suicide, and they are tasked with keeping us in darkness and holding us captive to it. You may or may not be affected by them all or exactly the same way as someone else; but I find it extremely necessary and crucial to identify the light which is available to us all to overcome them with victory.

For whatever is born of God overcomes the world.
And this is the victory that has overcome the world – our faith.

1 John 5:4

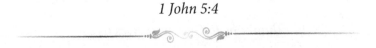

Before we move on to the light, I want to put on my 'Paul hat' and inform you that your victory will not happen overnight or just because you prayed and asked for victory. It really does not work like that at all, unfortunately, but we will receive our victory as promise.

There are many articles and books that discuss tactics to win over battles in the spiritual warfare. I found and witness these simple steps listed below to consider while patiently waiting on God's timing on our victories.

1. Identify the enemy and the current battle that is being faced. You cannot avoid your battles with the enemy. So address them and let them know you are aware of your fight and you will gain victory over them.

2. Pray to our Lord and Savior Jesus Christ. It is necessary to have full communication to the one that can and will bring victory over us.

3. Stand firm with the tools and weapons that are provided to us. This is the time to put on the full Armor of God.

4. Lastly but most importantly have faith. Our faith is very powerful and strong, it will change the course of our lives for the good of the Lord, even while waiting on our victory.

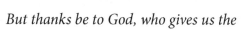

But thanks be to God, who gives us the

victory through our Lord Jesus Christ.

1 Corinthians 15:57

CHAPTER 5

THE LIGHT

Again, a new commandment I write to you, which thing is true in Him and in you, because the darkness is passing away, and the true light is already shining.

1 John 2:8

Light can be defined as something which makes vision possible, something that enlightens or informs, as well as to bring a particular aspect or appearance presented to view. It can also be known as a set of principles, standards, or opinions from a noteworthy person. These meanings can apply to our spiritual understanding of God's Light. His truth will make vision possible, enlighten and inform us on all things; and presents to us the appropriate aspects to view matters, that we come across on our journeys. God has also sent the only noteworthy person to set the principles and standards of living for the journey of life.

*This is the message which we have heard
from him and declare to you:*

God is light; in him there is no darkness at all.

*If we claim to have fellowship with him
and yet walk in the darkness,*

*We lie and do not live out the truth. But if we
walk in the light, as he is in the light,*

*We have fellowship with one another, and the blood
of Jesus, his Son, purifies us from all sin.*

1 John 1:5-7

God's light for us is simply seeking His truth and believing in His word on that truth. With that being said let us turn to the bible for some light and truth on suicide:

Wherefore I say unto you, All manner of sin and

blasphemy shall be forgiven unto men: but the blasphemy

against the Holy Ghost shall not be forgiven unto men.

And whosoever speaketh a word against the Son of

Man, it shall be forgiven him: but whosoever speaketh

against the Holy Ghost it shall not be forgiven him,

neither in this world, neither in the world to come.

Matthew 12:31-32 (KJV)

The unforgivable sin is blasphemy against the Spirit; which means that all sin can be forgiven except for speaking against the Holy Spirit. Suicide is not an unforgivable sin and can be forgiven by God. As I mentioned previously suicide is a weapon that the enemy uses in his attacks against God's children.

There are at least seven suicides mentioned in the bible. I notice that they steamed from either pride, distress, hopelessness, terror, revenge, rejection, guilt, and/or some form of burden. It is evident that when these emotions are not addressed or dismissed the enemy will use them to attack the individual that harbors them. The person is left to feel like he or she can take matters into their own hands to solve the situation and circumstance in which they are encountering during this specific season of their life.

The enemy's tactic is to make us believe that there is no end to our suffering, no hope for our situation, this is only happening because of something we did and we are all alone, or place any manipulative thought to the person as a way to defeat them in their battle. These are all lies of the enemy, and we must remember this when we are under attack.

The only way to get to the root of these emotions and lies are to seek the truth of them through the Lord. Our decisions are dependent on those thoughts and will be the factor to the outcomes and results of our actions. Those actions will be based on truths or lies, lightness or darkness, good or evil, or whatever combination you prefer to get the overall point of this matter.

Oh send out Your light and Your truth!

Let them lead me; Let them bring me to Your holy hill

And to Your tabernacle.

Psalms 43:3-4

Light for the Loss Survivor:

He performs wonders that cannot be fathomed,

miracles that cannot be counted.

When he passes me, I cannot see him;

When he goes by, I cannot perceive him.

If he snatches away, who can stop him?

Who can say to him 'What are you doing?'

Job 9:10-12 (NIV)

How then can I dispute with him?

How can I find words to argue with him?

Though I were innocent, I could not answer him;

I could only plead with my judge for mercy.

Job 9:14-15 (NIV)

As loss survivors, we debate with questions like those mention in the scriptures. Unfortunately, in times of loss like ours, we misplace our emotions on God, ourselves, and others who we believe could have change the outcomes of the actions of our loved ones. I believe God gets hit the hardest with blame out of us all with not preventing this from happening from someone in which we truly love.

Some of us turn from Him, become rebellious, even speak from a place of anger and pain on our feelings and thoughts towards Him as our God. Some of us turn the event of this loss as a punishment or injustice for ourselves. During our season of grieving and accepting our loss, we must remember God's justice, goodness, majesty, and condemnation away from any self-righteousness.

All of this will assist us with seeing God's Light in our personal experience with this tragedy in which we have to encounter with the loss of suicide. Only God can provide us with the comfort and knowledge; we need to move forward on this path that has been included to our journey of life.

There will be no short cuts on these paths, but just know that God is there and will provide, heal, and restore all of that and more to us as we endure this part of our journey. Cherish the love, memories, and time that you had and will continue to have for your loved ones. There is no enemy that can ever take that away from you. May God send you peace and comfort in your times of needs always and forever sealed with love.

The people living in darkness have seen a great light,

On those living in the land of the shadow of death

A light has dawned.

Matthew 4:16 (NIV)

Light for those in the Battle:

Your battle is real and is pulling you deeper into darkness. A darkness that no man can understand or shed light on. It makes you feel all alone in this fight; the attacks are getting stronger with no end at sight. Your worst option begins to present itself as the best option to end your battle.

Although there is no mankind to fully know and understand your exact fight with darkness. You have a Lord that turns darkness into light. He will take over your fight if you just trust in Him. That's right, you will not need to fight in this battle. You will position yourself, stand still, and see the salvation of the Lord who is always with you.

God loves you and there is nothing that can change that fact. He will be your hiding place. He shall preserve you from trouble and surround you with songs of deliverance. I pray that you lean on God to break you free from all of your strongholds and have faith that He will release you, and win your battle with total victory. In the mighty name of Jesus, I pray Amen.

In the same way, let your light shine before others,

That they may see your good deeds

And glorify your Father in Heaven

Matthew 5:16 (NIV)

It is extremely important that we share our light with others. We will come across millions of people on our paths of life. Our testimonies of God's Light whether as a survivor of the loss or a victor that has overcome their battle, it can be used for those that are currently suffering and battling against this enemy. As I mentioned several times throughout this book that all of us have unique experiences and stories pertaining to this matter; and I believe that God has assigned people to each of us that needs to hear that light that shines from them.

Dr. Freedenthal said it best when she stated that "there is an entire movement of people who have lost a loved one to suicide and who, in turn, are dedicated to helping others who find themselves in the same tragic situation; and with openness people find a community of others who can normalize the experience, who can offer hope and healing, and who welcome them with acceptance."

It was through this community of people, where I found the comfort and support that I desperately wanted and needed.

I did not have to explain or share anything to anyone, just being in their presence alone was enough for me. God opened my eyes to see the light.

His light through their stories which gave me hope. This was an undeniable hope for my own story. It was truly amazing to witness someone with almost the same exact story and experience as myself turn the pain and sorrow into something special such as a movie to contribute to the prevention of suicide.

At that moment God provided me with this truth, I was not alone and this did not just happen to me. There were people in this world who understood exactly what I was going through even when I didn't have the words to express and explain it to them.

We are all survivors. Whether we are coping with the loss of a loved one or battling against the attacks, either way, we are surviving the warfare of suicide and together we can bring light for our community. I have included contact information for some important resources in our community, which are available to assist us at the end of the book.

As this chapter comes to an end, I will close with stating that many of God's children have fallen due to this weapon. The rise of its attacks are crucial to those living in this era. God loves his children just like any other parent. He is commanding His light to shine on the hearts of those who have been affected by these attacks and battles. This will prevent his children from losing out on an opportunity to walk and live their lives to the fullest.

CHAPTER 6

THE LOVE

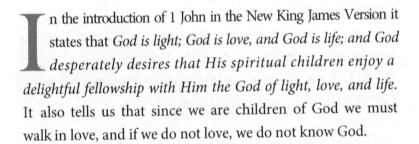

For you were once darkness, but now you are light in the Lord.

Walk as children of light.

Ephesians 5:8

In the introduction of 1 John in the New King James Version it states that *God is light; God is love, and God is life; and God desperately desires that His spiritual children enjoy a delightful fellowship with Him the God of light, love, and life.* It also tells us that since we are children of God we must walk in love, and if we do not love, we do not know God.

In order to fully walk in this love, we must realize that our standards of love is not the same as God's love. We have to consider that we all have our own perspectives and experiences of what love is to us. This causes us to put conditions on our understanding and meaning of love.

God's word will give us a clear understanding of His love, so we can know Him as the true God of Love. There are many scriptures throughout the entire Bible that teaches us all about God's love. I will point a few of them out in this chapter, but I want to focus on what the introduction of 1 John tells us about love. It states that love is more than just words; it is actions. Love is giving, not getting.

Biblical love is unconditional in its nature. Christ's love fulfilled those qualities and when that brand of love characterizes us, we will be free of self-condemnation and experience confidence before God. God's love will conform our character to have confidence in Him, so that we do not condemn ourselves; but rather trust and have faith in His plan for our journeys of life.

This does not mean we will not encounter tribulations during our journeys, but we will have glory in them. Romans 5:3-5 states that *we also glory in tribulations, knowing that tribulation produces perseverance; and perseverance, character; and character, hope. Now hope does not disappoint because the love of God has been poured out in our hearts by the Holy Spirit who was given to us.* There is something soothing about knowing this fact of God's love being poured into our hearts.

Our hearts can fail us at times, and I believe that is why 1 John 3:18-21 tells us *not to love in word or in tongue, but indeed and in truth. And by this we know that we are of the truth and shall assure our hearts before Him. For if our heart condemns us, God is greater than our heart, and knows all things. Beloved, if our heart does not condemn us, we have confidence toward God.*

Here is another comforting truth about God's love for us from 1 John 4:12-15:

"If we love one another God abides in us, and His love has been perfected in us. By this we know that we abide in Him, and He in us, because He has given us of His Spirit. And we have seen and testify that the Father has sent the Son as Savior of the world. Whoever confesses that Jesus is the Son of God, God abides in Him, and he in God. And we have known and believed the love that God has for us. God is love, and he who abides in love abides in God, and God in him."

It is amazing how God's love will equip us with so much and more to live out our journeys and the paths we venture through during our lifetime. The love of God can be used in our battles and fights. It will give us confidence and security, and provide us with comfort and peace to endure this warfare.

I want to break that down a little more for you, so you can truly know the power of God's love that is placed inside of us. It is so important to remember that when you are in battle and in a fight on your journey that God's love ensures us that God is with us.

Deuteronomy 20:4 tells *us that when we are on the verge of battle with our enemies to not let our heart faint, be afraid, tremble, or be terrified because of them; for the Lord your God is He who goes with you, to fight for you against your enemies, to save you.* Yes, God is going to be with you during your battles and you are going to have victory over them all.

It is also imperative that we have Godly confidence for these journeys of life that have been given to us. Proverbs 3:26 states that *For the Lord will be your confidence, and will keep your foot from being caught.* This is explaining to us that our Godly confidence with the love of God will bring us a security that will keep us from getting stuck in any tunnels of darkness that happens to come across our path.

Job 11:17 reminds us that *though you were dark, you will be like the morning. And you would be secure, because there is hope; yes, you dig around you, and take your rest in safety.* Our safety is found in our hope in God to secure us at all times. We are now able to take our rest in knowing this truth for us.

Paul tells us in 2 Corinthians 13:11 *to become complete, be of good comfort, be of one mind, live in peace; and the God of love and peace will be with us.* That is our formula to fully receive the love of God and peace for our lives and journeys.

As I move forward from this please keep this in your heart always:

For I am persuaded that neither death nor life, nor angels nor

Principalities nor powers, nor things present nor things to come,

Nor height nor depth, nor any other created thing,

Shall be able to separate us from the

Love of God which is in Christ Jesus our Lord.

Romans 8:38-39

We will never know the last moment in which our loved ones had with the Lord. However, I truly believe that the Lord spoke something like this to them all:

My child this is not my will for you, and I can get you out of this and through this if you trust Me; it won't be easy, painless, or simple. You may be prosecuted and afflicted, but if you choose to make this decision, I will still love you and bring light out of your darkness by the seeds you have planted on your journey. Beloved, I know you are brokenhearted, oppressed, and troubled with no sight to an end. I am with you and love you always. This is your decision my child, and I am here with you.

I will end this chapter and bring closure to this book with this fact; there is nothing, absolutely nothing that can separate us from the love of God. This includes suicide and the attempts of suicide. God loves us just the way we are; even with the situations and circumstances that we have brought upon ourselves. He is the only one that truly knows us, even better than we know ourselves. Psalms 139 breaks down just how much God knows us, and shows that his love is truly unconditional for us.

God has given us a way to be forgiven for all of our sins. He will bring clarity to us if we believe, have faith, and trust in Him. God will supply all of our needs and more. He does all of this for one reason, and it is because God loves us. I pray, as you journey through this life you keep hold of God's love and remember you are His light to the darkness of this world. Shine bright my siblings; in Jesus' name. Amen.

But You are a chosen generation,

A royal priesthood, a holy nation,

His own special people, that proclaim the praises of Him

Who called you out of darkness into His marvelous light;

Who once were not a people but are now the people of God,

Who had not obtained mercy but now have obtained mercy.

1 Peter 2:9-10

<u>Community Information</u>

American Foundation for Suicide Prevention (AFSP)

Website: https://afsp.org/

AFSP Loss Survivor

Website: https://afsp.org/find-support/ive-lost-someone/

National Suicide Prevention Lifeline

Telephone Number: 1-800-273-TALK (8255)

Crisis Text Line by texting TALK to 741741

REFERENCES

I. Grace to You by John MacArthur

II. Total Surrender Message by Billy Graham

III. Blindsided by Suicide by Linda Kipley

IV. The Wounded Child's Journey into Love's Embrace by Paul Ferrini

V. *Shame Fester in Dark Place: Keeping Suicide Secret* by Dr. Stacey Freedenthal

VI. *Battling the Unbelief of Misplaced Shame by* Pastor John Piper

VII. *Conversations with God-an uncommon dialogue, Book 1* by Neale Donald Walsch

VIII. *Conversations with God-an uncommon dialogue, Book 2* by Neale Donald Walsch

ABOUT THE AUTHOR

Mia Wallace was born and raised in Washington, DC and its metropolitan area. She currently lives in Atlanta, GA with her son. Along with being a single mother, Ms. Wallace is a full-time Management Analyst for the Centers for Disease Control and Prevention, the CEO of Travel Elevation LLC, and the CEO and Founder of Kingdom Powerhouse LLC.

She enjoys traveling, swimming, reading, spending time with family, and serving the Lord. In this new season of her life, God has given her the urge to write the amazing things that He has placed in her heart to share with the world. You can expect more from this Christian author.

Ms. Wallace can be reached at the email listed below for any: speaking engagements, interviews, and/or appearance events.

Email: officialmiawallace@gmail.com

She can also be found on the following Social Media Platforms:

Facebook & Instagram: officialmiawallace

Twitter: 1officialmiaw

Made in the USA
Columbia, SC
05 August 2019